THE SECURITY CAMERA HANDBOOK

PLANNING, IMPLEMENTATION, AND PREPAREDNESS FOR A SAFE HOME

L.G. SCHREYER

Copyright © [2024] by [L.G. Schreyer]

All rights reserved.

No portion of this book may be reproduced in any form without written permission from the publisher or author, except as permitted by U.S. copyright law.

Contents

Introduction: Your Path to a Secure Home   1
1. Chapter 1: The Basics of Security Camera Placement   2
2. Chapter 2: Home Layout and Camera Mapping   12
3. Chapter 3: Installing Your Security Cameras   18
4. Chapter 4: Recording Options for Security Cameras   24
5. Chapter 5: Maintenance and Troubleshooting   32
6. Chapter 6: Exploring Advanced Features and Integrations   38
7. Chapter 7: Creating a Comprehensive Security Plan   45
8. Chapter 8: Staying Vigilant and Proactive in Home Security   53
9. Chapter 9: Responding to Security Breaches and Emergencies   60

Conclusion   66

Introduction: Your Path to a Secure Home

Welcome to "The Security Camera Handbook: Planning, Implementation, and Preparedness for a Safe Home." Ensuring the safety and security of our homes has never been more important in today's world. With the rise in residential burglaries and the growing need for peace of mind, a robust security system is essential. Strategically placed security cameras are one of the most effective components of any home security system. They act as both a deterrent to potential intruders and a critical tool in monitoring and protecting your property.

This guide is designed to assist you in making informed decisions about the placement, maintenance, and integration of your security cameras. Whether you are a homeowner looking to enhance your current security setup or a first-time security system installer, this guide provides comprehensive and practical information to help you achieve optimal coverage and protection.

Chapter 1: The Basics of Security Camera Placement

The Power of Proper Camera Placement

In your quest for a secure home, strategically placing security cameras becomes one of the most critical steps. While the mere presence of cameras can deter would-be intruders, their effectiveness dramatically increases when you position them correctly. Properly placed cameras provide comprehensive coverage of your property, capturing crucial details that could prove vital in preventing or solving security incidents.

This chapter will introduce you to the fundamental principles of security camera placement. You will learn about the types of cameras available, the areas of your home that require monitoring, and common mistakes to avoid. By the end of this chapter, you will have a solid understanding of how to place your cameras for maximum effectiveness.

Types of Security Cameras

Before diving into placement strategies, it's essential to understand the different types of security cameras available. Each type has its own features and is suited for specific purposes:

Dome Cameras

- **Features:** Dome cameras have a dome-shaped housing, providing a sleek and discreet appearance. They are typically mounted on ceilings and offer a wide-angle view, making them ideal for covering large areas. Many dome cameras come with vandal-resistant and weatherproof features, enhancing their durability.

- **Best For:** Indoor use, particularly in large rooms or areas that require broad coverage, such as living rooms, hallways, and retail spaces.

- **Installation Difficulty:** Moderate to Hard. Installing dome cameras involves mounting on the ceiling, which may require drilling and securing brackets. Running power and communication wires, adjusting angles, and ensuring a stable network connection add complexity.

Bullet Cameras

- **Features:** Bullet cameras are long and cylindrical, designed to be highly visible, which can deter intruders. They often feature a robust and durable design, with weatherproof and infrared capabilities for night vision, making them suitable for outdoor use.

- **Best For:** Outdoor surveillance, especially in areas requiring long-distance viewing, such as driveways, backyards, and parking lots.

- **Installation Difficulty:** Moderate to Hard. Installing bullet cameras involves mounting on walls or eaves, which requires drilling, securing brackets, and running power and network cables, especially at higher elevations.

PTZ Cameras (Pan-Tilt-Zoom)

- **Features:** PTZ cameras can pan, tilt, and zoom, providing comprehensive coverage and flexibility to focus on specific details. These cameras often come with advanced features like motion tracking and presets for automated surveillance.

- **Best For:** Large, open spaces that need versatile and dynamic monitoring, such as warehouses, large yards, and commercial properties.

- **Installation Difficulty:** High. PTZ cameras require careful mounting and connection to both power and control systems. Configuring the pan, tilt, and zoom functions, often via software, adds complexity. Professional installation is recommended.

Doorbell Cameras

- **Features:** Integrated into doorbells, these cameras offer video and audio communication with visitors, allowing homeowners to see and speak with anyone at their door via a smartphone app. Many models include motion detection and night vision.

- **Best For:** Monitoring front doors and entryways, providing both security and convenience.

- **Installation Difficulty:** Low to Moderate. Doorbell cameras can replace existing doorbells using existing wiring. Wireless models simplify installation but require careful positioning to ensure strong Wi-Fi connectivity.

Wireless Cameras

- **Features:** Wireless cameras connect to your network without extensive wiring, offering flexibility in placement. Batteries or a power adapter can power these cameras, and many include features like cloud storage and remote access.

- **Best For:** Flexible installation in areas where running cables would be difficult, such as rental properties, temporary setups, or locations far from power sources.

- **Installation Difficulty:** Low. Wireless cameras are typically easy to install, requiring only mounting and configuration to the home network. Ensuring strong Wi-Fi signals and managing battery replacements or recharges can add minor challenges.

Hidden Cameras

Features: Designed to be inconspicuous, hidden cameras blend into the environment, appearing as everyday objects like clocks, smoke detectors, or picture frames. They provide discreet monitoring without alerting potential intruders.

- **Best For:** Discreet monitoring of specific areas inside the home, such as nurseries, home offices, or living areas where covert surveillance is desired.

- **Installation Difficulty:** Low to Moderate. Hidden cameras often come pre-installed in everyday objects, making placement straightforward. Ensuring they have a clear view and managing their power and data connections can be slightly more complex.

Key Areas to Monitor

Effective security camera placement involves covering all critical areas of your property. Here are some of the most important locations to consider:

Front Door
- **Why:** The front door is the main entry point for most homes. Monitoring this area helps capture visitors, deliveries,

and potential intruders.

Back and Side Doors
- **Why:** Intruders often target these doors for less visible entry points.

Windows
- **Why:** Ground-floor windows are common entry points for burglars. Cameras should cover these vulnerable spots.

Driveways and Garages
- **Why:** Monitoring these areas helps protect vehicles and provides an early warning of approaching visitors or intruders.

Yard and Perimeter
- **Why:** Outdoor cameras can deter intruders before they reach the home and give a broader view of the property.

Common Areas
- **Why:** Indoor cameras placed in common areas like living rooms or hallways can help monitor activity inside the home.

Common Placement Mistakes to Avoid

While the goal is to achieve comprehensive coverage, it's easy to make mistakes in camera placement. Here are some common pitfalls to avoid:

Ignoring Lighting Conditions
- **Mistake:** Placing cameras in areas with poor lighting or direct sunlight can affect image quality.

- **Solution:** Ensure cameras are equipped with night vision for low-light areas and are positioned to avoid direct sunlight.

Creating Blind Spots
- **Mistake:** Failing to overlap camera views can leave gaps in coverage.

- **Solution:** Plan camera placement to ensure overlapping fields of view and eliminate blind spots.

Mounting Cameras Too High or Too Low
- **Mistake:** Cameras placed too high may miss facial details, while those too low can be easily tampered with.

- **Solution:** Mount cameras at a height that balances security and image detail, typically around 8-10 feet.

Neglecting Wireless Signal Strength
- **Mistake:** Wireless cameras placed too far from the router may suffer from weak signal and connectivity issues.

- **Solution:** Ensure wireless cameras are within range of your router or use signal boosters if necessary.

Overlooking Regular Maintenance
- **Mistake:** Neglecting to clean and maintain cameras can degrade image quality over time.

- **Solution:** Establish a regular maintenance schedule to keep cameras in optimal condition.

Conclusion

The strategic placement of security cameras is vital to any home security system. You can significantly enhance your home's security by understanding the different types of cameras available, identifying key areas to monitor, and avoiding common placement mistakes. The subsequent chapters of this guide will provide you with detailed templates, checklists, and logs to help you plan, install, and maintain your security cameras effectively.

Let's move on to Chapter 2, where we will dive into the practical steps of mapping out your home and planning your camera placements. We will create a comprehensive security plan to protect your home and loved ones.

Chapter 2: Home Layout and Camera Mapping

Mapping Out Your Home for Optimal Coverage

Properly mapping out your home is a critical first step in strategically placing security cameras. A well-thought-out layout will help ensure that every vulnerable area is covered, eliminating blind spots and maximizing the effectiveness of your security system. In this chapter, we will guide you through creating a detailed map of your property, planning camera placements, and documenting key details.

Step 1: Sketch Your Home Layout

Start by drawing a simple floor plan of your home. You don't need to be an artist; a basic sketch will suffice. Include the following elements in your layout:

Entry Points:
- Front door
- Back door
- Side doors
- Garage doors

Windows:
- Ground floor windows
- Basement windows
- Any accessible windows on the upper floors

Outdoor Areas:
- Driveways

- Walkways

- Yards (front, back, and sides)

- Patios and decks

Indoor Areas:
- Common areas (living room, kitchen, hallways)

- High-value rooms (home office, master bedroom)

- Staircases

Perimeter Fencing and Gates:
- Any fences or gates surrounding your property

Once you have a basic sketch, make several copies. You will use these copies to plan the placement of your security cameras.

Step 2: Identify Key Coverage Areas

Next, identify the key areas that need coverage. These are typically locations where intruders are most likely to enter or areas that require constant monitoring. Key areas include:

Entry and Exit Points:
- Ensure that all doors and accessible windows are covered.

- Front door cameras should capture visitors' faces and any packages left at the doorstep.

Driveways and Parking Areas:
- Cover these areas to monitor vehicles and any activity around them.

Backyard and Side Yards:
- Place cameras to cover secluded areas that might be attractive to intruders.

Perimeter and Fence Lines:
- Install cameras along the property lines to monitor for any unauthorized access.

Indoor High-Value Areas:
- Place cameras in rooms with valuables or sensitive information, such as home offices or master bedrooms.

Common Indoor Areas:
- Monitor common areas and hallways to track movement within the house.

Step 3: Plan Camera Placement

With your key coverage areas identified, you can now plan where to place each camera. Use the following guidelines to help with placement:

Front Door:
- Position the camera at eye level to capture clear images of faces.
- Consider a doorbell camera for video and audio communication with visitors.

Back and Side Doors:
- Mount cameras above doors to capture anyone entering or leaving.

- Ensure the camera angle covers the entire doorway.

Windows:
- Place cameras to cover ground-level windows.
- Avoid placing cameras directly facing windows to prevent glare.

Driveways and Garages:
- Position cameras to cover the entire driveway and any vehicles.
- Ensure the camera angle includes the garage door.

Yard and Perimeter:
- Place cameras high enough to cover large areas but low enough to capture details.
- Ensure cameras are equipped with night vision for low-light areas and are positioned to avoid direct sunlight.

Indoor Areas:
- Place cameras in corners to cover the largest area.
- Ensure cameras are discreet and not easily tampered with.

Step 4: Document Camera Details

For each planned camera location, document the following details on your layout:
- **Camera Type:** Specify the type of camera (dome, bullet, PTZ, doorbell, wireless, hidden).

- **Field of View:** Note the expected field of view and any areas of overlap with other cameras.

- **Installation Height:** Record the planned installation height to ensure optimal coverage.

- **Power Source:** Identify the power source (wired, battery, solar) and any necessary cable runs.

- **Network Connectivity:** Ensure the camera location is within range of your Wi-Fi network or plan for wired connections.

Step 5: Review and Adjust

Review your planned camera placements to ensure comprehensive coverage. Look for potential blind spots or areas with overlapping coverage and adjust the placements as needed to optimize your property's security.

Conclusion

Creating a detailed map of your home and planning your camera placements is essential for a robust security system. Following the steps outlined in this chapter, you can ensure your cameras are strategically placed to provide maximum coverage and protection. The next chapter will delve into the installation process, offering tips and best practices to ensure a smooth and effective setup. Let's move forward confidently, knowing you are taking crucial steps to secure your home and loved ones.

Chapter 3: Installing Your Security Cameras

Preparing for Installation

Now that you have mapped out your home and planned the placement of your security cameras, it's time to move on to the installation process. Proper installation ensures that your cameras function effectively and provide the necessary coverage. In this chapter, we will guide you through installing your cameras, from gathering the necessary tools to configuring the system for optimal performance.

Step 1: Gather Your Tools and Equipment

Before you start, ensure you have all the tools and equipment needed for the installation. Here's a checklist to help you prepare:

- **Security Cameras:** Ensure you have all the cameras you plan to install, along with any mounting brackets and hardware.

- **Power Supply:** Check that you have the necessary power adapters, batteries, or solar panels for each camera.

- **Network Equipment:** Gather any necessary routers, Wi-Fi extenders, or Ethernet cables.

- **Mounting Tools:** Have a drill, screwdrivers, level, measuring tape, and screws/anchors appropriate for the surface where you'll mount the cameras.

- **Ladder:** A sturdy ladder is essential for mounting cameras at higher locations.

- **Cable Management:** Use zip ties, cable clips, or conduits to manage and conceal wiring.

- **Smartphone or Tablet:** This will be useful for configuring and testing your cameras during installation.

Step 2: Install the Mounting Brackets

Start by installing the mounting brackets for each camera. Follow these steps:

1. **Mark the Mounting Location:**

    - Use a pencil to mark the spots where you will drill holes for the mounting brackets.

    - Ensure the marks align with the positions you planned in Chapter 2.

2. **Drill Holes:**

    - Use a drill bit that matches the size of your screws/anchors to drill holes at the marked locations.

    - If mounting on brick or concrete, use masonry anchors.

3. **Attach the Brackets:**

    - Secure the mounting brackets to the wall or ceiling using the screws and anchors.

    - Use a level to ensure the brackets are straight.

Step 3: Mount the Cameras

Once the brackets are securely in place, you can mount the cameras:

1. **Attach the Camera:**

    - Align the camera with the mounting bracket and secure it according to the manufacturer's instructions.

- Ensure the camera is firmly attached and won't move or fall.

2. **Adjust the Angle:**

    - Adjust the camera angle to cover the desired area.
    - Use the camera's live feed on your smartphone or tablet to fine-tune the positioning.

Step 4: Connect the Power Supply

With the cameras mounted, it's time to connect the power supply:

- **Wired Cameras:**

    - Run the power cables from the camera to the nearest power outlet.
    - Use cable management tools to conceal and secure the wires.
    - Plug the camera into the power outlet.

- **Wireless Cameras:**

    - Insert batteries or connect the camera to its power adapter.
    - Ensure the camera is within range of your Wi-Fi network.

- **Solar-Powered Cameras:**

- Install the solar panel in a location with ample sunlight.

- Connect the solar panel to the camera using the provided cables.

Step 5: Configure the Cameras

After connecting the power supply, configure your cameras for optimal performance:

1. **Connect to the Network:**

   - Follow the manufacturer's instructions to connect each camera to your Wi-Fi network or Ethernet connection.

   - Ensure a strong and stable connection to prevent interruptions.

2. **Set Up the Software:**

   - Download and install the camera manufacturer's app on your smartphone or tablet.

   - Create an account and follow the prompts to add each camera to your system.

   - Configure settings such as motion detection, recording schedules, and alerts.

3. **Test the Cameras:**

   - Verify that each camera is working correctly by viewing the live feed on your app.

- Check the coverage area and adjust the angle if necessary.

- Test the motion detection and recording features to ensure they function as expected.

Step 6: Secure the System

Once your cameras are installed and configured, take steps to secure your system:

- **Change Default Passwords:** To enhance security, change any default passwords for your camera system to strong, unique passwords.

- **Enable Encryption:** Enable encryption features to protect your video feed from unauthorized access, if available.

- **Regular Updates:** Keep your camera firmware and app updated with the latest security patches and features.

Conclusion

Installing your security cameras correctly is vital to ensuring that your home is well-protected. You can achieve a smooth and effective installation by following the steps outlined in this chapter. Regularly test and adjust your cameras to maintain optimal coverage and performance.

In the next chapter, we will discuss recording options for your CCTV system. Let's continue building a safer home with confidence and diligence.

Chapter 4: Recording Options for Security Cameras

Capturing and Storing Footage for Maximum Security

Recording and storing footage is a vital aspect of any home security system. The right recording options ensure you capture critical events, review footage when needed, and maintain evidence for security incidents. This chapter will explore various recording options for security cameras, their benefits, and how to choose the best solution for your needs.

Types of Recording Options

Understanding the different recording options available will help you make an informed decision that fits your security needs and budget.

Local Storage:

- **Description:** Local storage involves saving video footage directly to a device on your property, such as a DVR (Digital Video Recorder) or NVR (Network Video Recorder). These devices usually have a set amount of cameras that can be added to them. Always plan for future expansion when choosing this option.

- **Benefits:**

    ○ No recurring fees.

    ○ Complete control over footage.

    ○ No reliance on internet connectivity.

- **Considerations:**

    ○ Limited storage capacity.

- Risk of theft or damage to the storage device.
- Requires regular maintenance to manage storage space.

Cloud Storage:

- **Description:** Cloud storage saves video footage to remote servers managed by a service provider.
- **Benefits:**
  - Access footage from anywhere with an internet connection.
  - Off-site storage protects against theft or damage.
  - Scalable storage options.
- **Considerations:**
  - Recurring subscription fees.
  - Dependence on internet connectivity for uploading and accessing footage.
  - Potential privacy concerns with third-party storage.

Hybrid Storage:

- **Description:** Hybrid storage combines local and cloud storage, allowing you to store footage on-site and remotely.

- **Benefits:**
  - Redundant storage ensures data safety.
  - Access footage locally and remotely.
  - Balances control and convenience.
- **Considerations:**
  - Higher costs due to maintaining both storage types.
  - Requires setup and management of both systems.

MicroSD Cards:

- **Description:** Some cameras offer built-in slots for microSD cards, allowing direct storage on the camera.
- **Benefits:**
  - Easy to set up and use.
  - No additional hardware is required.
  - Affordable storage option.
- **Considerations:**
  - Limited storage capacity.
  - Vulnerable to theft or damage.
  - Requires manual retrieval of footage.

Choosing the Right Recording Option

Selecting the best recording option depends on your specific needs, preferences, and budget. Consider the following factors:

Storage Capacity:
- Determine how much footage you need to store based on camera resolution, number of cameras, and desired retention period.
- Local storage devices and cloud plans offer varying capacities. Choose one that meets your requirements.

Access and Convenience:
- Decide how and where you want to access your footage. Cloud storage offers remote access, while local storage provides on-site access.
- Consider hybrid storage if you need the flexibility of both access types.

Cost:
- Evaluate your budget for initial setup and ongoing expenses.
- Local storage typically has a higher upfront cost but no recurring fees, while cloud storage involves subscription costs.

Security and Privacy:
- Assess the security measures of the storage solution. Ensure cloud providers offer encryption and strong privacy policies.
- Local storage keeps data on your property, providing more control over who can access it.

Redundancy and Reliability:
- Consider the reliability of your storage solution. Cloud storage offers protection against local device failures, while hybrid storage provides redundancy.

- Ensure regular backups if using local storage exclusively.

Configuring Your Recording System

Once you choose a recording option, properly configuring your system is essential for optimal performance.

Local Storage Configuration:
- **Setup:** Connect cameras to your DVR/NVR and configure settings such as resolution, frame rate, and recording schedule.

- **Management:** Regularly check storage capacity, delete old footage as needed, and perform backups.

Cloud Storage Configuration:
- **Setup:** Sign up for a cloud storage service and connect your cameras to the platform. Configure recording settings and storage plans.

- **Management:** Monitor your storage usage, upgrade plans if necessary, and ensure a stable internet connection for uninterrupted uploads.

Hybrid Storage Configuration:
- **Setup:** Set up both local and cloud storage systems, ensuring they are properly integrated.

- **Management:** Balance storage usage between local and cloud, perform regular backups and maintain both systems.

MicroSD Card Configuration:
- **Setup:** Insert microSD cards into cameras and configure recording settings.

- **Management:** Regularly check card capacity, replace cards as needed, and retrieve footage manually for review or backup.

Reviewing and Managing Footage

Efficiently reviewing and managing your footage is crucial for maintaining an effective security system.

Regular Reviews:
- Schedule regular checks of recorded footage to ensure your system is functioning correctly and capturing relevant events.

- Set up alerts and notifications for motion detection or specific events to review footage promptly.

Footage Management:
- Organize and label footage for easy retrieval. Use software tools to search, filter, and categorize videos.

- Regularly back up important footage to prevent loss and ensure data integrity.

Incident Handling:
- Develop a protocol for handling security incidents. Know

how to retrieve and export footage for evidence.

- Share relevant footage with authorities or insurance companies as needed.

Conclusion

Choosing the right recording option for your security cameras ensures comprehensive coverage and easy access to footage. You can create a reliable and efficient recording solution by understanding the different recording options, considering your specific needs, and properly configuring your system. Regularly review and manage your footage to maintain an effective security system and respond promptly to incidents.

In the next chapter, we will discuss maintenance and troubleshooting to help you keep your security system running smoothly. Let's continue building a safer home with confidence and diligence.

Chapter 5: Maintenance and Troubleshooting

Keeping Your Security System in Top Shape

Maintaining your security cameras is essential to ensure they function effectively and provide reliable protection for your home. Regular maintenance and prompt troubleshooting can prevent issues before they become serious problems. This chapter will guide you through the best practices for maintaining your cameras and offer solutions to common issues that may arise.

Step 1: Regular Maintenance

Routine maintenance is crucial for the longevity and reliability of your security cameras. Here's a checklist to help you keep your system in top condition:

- **Cleaning the Cameras:**

    - **Frequency:** Clean the camera lenses at least once a month.

    - **Method:** Use a soft, dry cloth or lens cleaner to remove dust, dirt, and smudges. You may need a gentle cleaning solution for outdoor cameras to remove more stubborn grime.

- **Inspecting the Mounts and Cables:**

    - **Frequency:** Check mounts and cables every three months.

    - **Method:** Ensure the camera mounts are secure and have not been tampered with or damaged. Inspect cables for any wear, fraying, or exposure to the elements.

- **Checking Power Supplies:**

    - **Frequency:** Monthly for battery-operated cameras; quarterly for wired cameras.

    - **Method:** Ensure that all cameras are receiving power. For battery-operated cameras, replace or recharge batteries as needed. For wired cameras, check that power adapters are functioning correctly.

- **Testing the Network Connection:**

    - **Frequency:** Quarterly

    - **Method:** Ensure that each camera is connected to your

network and that the connection is stable. Check for any connectivity issues that might affect performance.

- **Reviewing Camera Angles:**

  - **Frequency:** Quarterly

  - **Method:** Verify that each camera is still covering the intended area. Adjust angles if necessary to account for environmental changes, such as growing vegetation or new structures.

Step 2: Troubleshooting Common Issues

Even with regular maintenance, you may encounter issues with your security cameras. Here are some common problems and their solutions:

- **Blurry or Distorted Images:**

  - **Cause:** Dirty lenses, incorrect focus, or camera damage.

  - **Solution:** Clean the lens, adjust the focus, and inspect the camera for physical damage.

- **No Video Feed:**

  - **Cause:** Power supply issues, network connectivity problems, or software glitches.

  - **Solution:** Check the power supply, ensure the camera is connected to the network, and restart the camera. If the issue persists, update the camera firmware or app.

- **Intermittent Video Feed:**
    - **Cause:** Weak Wi-Fi signal, interference, or network congestion.
    - **Solution:** Ensure the camera is within range of your router, reduce interference from other devices, or consider using a Wi-Fi extender.

- **False Motion Alerts:**
    - **Cause:** Sensitivity settings are too high or environmental factors like moving branches or shadows.
    - **Solution:** Adjust the motion sensitivity settings and reposition the camera to minimize false triggers.

- **Night Vision Issues:**
    - **Cause:** Infrared (IR) lights are obstructed, there are dirty lenses, or there is an inadequate power supply.
    - **Solution:** Clean the lenses, check the IR lights for obstructions, and ensure the camera receives sufficient power.

- **App Connectivity Problems:**
    - **Cause:** Software bugs, outdated apps, or network issues.
    - **Solution:** Update the camera app, restart your device, and ensure your network is functioning properly.

Step 3: Recording Maintenance and Troubleshooting

Keeping detailed records of your maintenance and troubleshooting activities helps track the performance of your security system and identify recurring issues. Use a maintenance log to document the following:

- **Date of Maintenance:** Record the date of each maintenance activity.

- **Tasks Performed:** List the tasks completed, such as cleaning lenses, inspecting mounts, or testing the network connection.

- **Issues Identified:** Note any problems discovered during maintenance.

- **Actions Taken:** Document the steps taken to resolve any issues.

- **Next Maintenance Date:** Schedule the next maintenance check.

Step 4: When to Call a Professional

While many maintenance and troubleshooting tasks can be handled on your own, some situations may require professional assistance:

- **Complex Installations:** A professional installer can ensure everything is set up correctly if your system involves advanced features like PTZ cameras, integrated alarm systems, or extensive cabling.

- **Persistent Issues:** If you encounter recurring problems that troubleshooting does not resolve, a professional can diagnose and fix the underlying issues.

- **Upgrades and Expansions:** Professional guidance can help you seamlessly integrate new equipment with your existing setup when upgrading your system or adding new components.

Conclusion

Regular maintenance and timely troubleshooting are essential to keeping your security cameras functioning at their best. By following the guidelines in this chapter, you can ensure your system remains reliable and effective in protecting your home. Documenting your maintenance activities and knowing when to seek professional help further enhance the longevity and performance of your security system.

The next chapter will explore advanced features and integrations to help you get the most out of your security system. Let's continue to build a safer, more secure home together.

Chapter 6: Exploring Advanced Features and Integrations

Maximizing Your Security System's Potential

Modern security systems have various advanced features and integration capabilities that can significantly enhance your home's protection. Understanding and utilizing these features can help you get the most out of your security system. This chapter will explore these advanced features and how to integrate them with other smart home devices to create a comprehensive and cohesive security network.

Step 1: Understanding Advanced Camera Features

Many security cameras offer advanced features that can improve surveillance capabilities. Here are some key features to look out for and how to use them effectively:

- **Motion Detection:**

    - How It Works: Cameras with motion detection can trigger alerts or start recording when they detect movement.

    - Benefits: Reduces the footage you must review by recording only when activity is detected.

    - Tips for Use: Adjust sensitivity settings to avoid false alarms caused by pets or environmental factors.

- **Two-Way Audio:**

    - How It Works: Allows you to listen and speak through the camera using your smartphone or tablet.

    - Benefits: Enables real-time communication with visitors or potential intruders.

    - Tips for Use: Use this feature to greet visitors, instruct delivery personnel, or deter intruders by letting them know they are being watched.

- **Facial Recognition:**

    - How It Works: Identifies and distinguishes between known and unknown individuals.

    - Benefits: Enhances security by alerting you to the presence of strangers.

- **Tips for Use:** Regularly update the database of known individuals to improve accuracy.

- **Geofencing:**

  - **How It Works:** Uses your smartphone's location to trigger actions such as turning on cameras when you leave home.

  - **Benefits:** Automates security measures based on your location.

  - **Tips for Use:** Set up geofencing to activate your security system automatically when you leave and deactivate it when you return.

- **Cloud Storage:**

  - **How It Works:** Stores recorded footage on remote servers instead of local devices.

  - **Benefits:** Provides secure storage and easy access to footage from anywhere.

  - **Tips for Use:** Choose a cloud storage plan that meets your needs and ensure your footage is encrypted for added security.

Step 2: Integrating with Smart Home Devices

Integrating your security cameras with other smart home devices can create a more comprehensive and automated security system. Here are some common smart home integrations:

- **Smart Lights:**

    - **Integration:** Connect your security cameras to smart lights that turn on when motion is detected.

    - **Benefits:** Illuminates potential intruders and enhances camera footage quality at night.

    - **Tips for Use:** Set up schedules or use motion detection to control the lights automatically.

- **Smart Locks:**

    - **Integration:** Pair your cameras with smart locks to see who is at your door and control the lock remotely.

    - **Benefits:** Adds a layer of security by allowing you to verify visitors before granting access.

    - **Tips for Use:** Use the camera's two-way audio to communicate with visitors and unlock the door if necessary.

- **Smart Doorbells:**

    - **Integration:** Combine your doorbell camera with other security cameras for a full view of your entryway.

    - **Benefits:** Provides comprehensive coverage and the ability to interact with visitors from anywhere.

    - **Tips for Use:** Sync your doorbell camera with indoor

cameras to track visitors throughout your home.

- **Home Automation Systems:**

    - **Integration:** Use platforms like Amazon Alexa, Google Home, or Apple HomeKit to control your security system with voice commands or automated routines.

    - **Benefits:** Simplifies control and integrates security with other home automation features.

    - **Tips for Use:** Create routines that activate your security cameras when you say specific phrases or when certain conditions are met (e.g. when you leave home).

Step 3: Enhancing Security with Advanced Monitoring

Advanced monitoring services can provide additional layers of security and peace of mind. Consider these options:

- **Professional Monitoring:**

    - **How It Works:** Security professionals monitor your system 24/7 and respond to alerts.

    - **Benefits:** Provides immediate response to emergencies, even when you're not available.

    - **Tips for Use:** Choose a reputable monitoring service and ensure they have quick response times and reliable communication channels.

- **Self-Monitoring:**

- **How It Works:** You receive alerts and monitor your system yourself through a mobile app.

- **Benefits:** Gives you direct control over your security and can be more cost-effective.

- **Tips for Use:** Ensure you have a reliable internet connection and stay vigilant about checking alerts.

• **Remote Access and Control:**

- **How It Works:** Access and control your security system from anywhere using a smartphone or tablet.

- **Benefits:** Allows you to monitor your home and respond to real-time alerts regardless of location.

- **Tips for Use:** Regularly update your app and security settings to protect against unauthorized access.

Step 4: Keeping Your System Updated

Regular updates and maintenance are essential to keep your security system functioning optimally:

• **Firmware and Software Updates:**

- **Importance:** Updates often include new features, security enhancements, and bug fixes.

- **Tips for Use:** If available, enable automatic updates or regularly check for updates through your camera's app or manufacturer's website.

- **Security Settings:**
  - **Importance:** Keeping your security settings up-to-date helps protect against unauthorized access.
  - **Tips for Use:** Use strong, unique passwords and enable two-factor authentication if available.

Conclusion

Advanced features and smart home integrations can significantly enhance your security system's effectiveness and convenience. By understanding these features and how to use them, you can create a more secure and automated home environment. Regular updates and vigilant monitoring further ensure your system remains reliable and effective.

The next chapter will discuss strategies for creating a comprehensive security plan tailored to your home's unique needs. Together, we will continue building a safer and more secure home.

Chapter 7: Creating a Comprehensive Security Plan

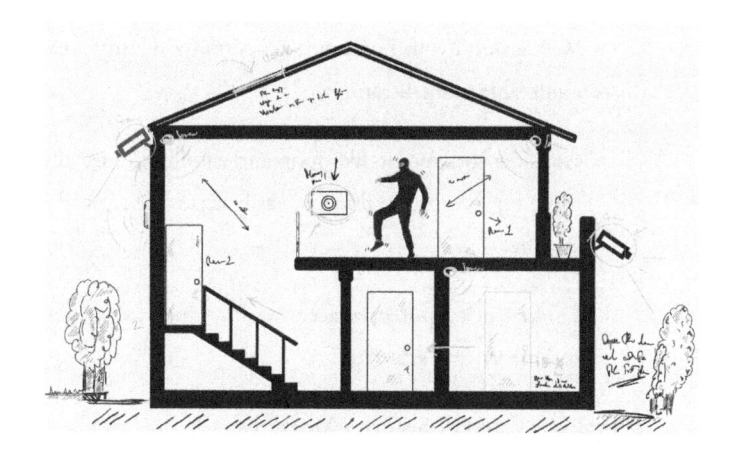

Designing a Security Strategy Tailored to Your Home

A comprehensive security plan is essential for ensuring the safety of your home and family. This plan involves assessing your home's unique needs, identifying potential vulnerabilities, and implementing effective security measures. This chapter will guide you through creating a tailored security plan that integrates all aspects of your security system.

Step 1: Assessing Your Home's Security Needs

The first step in creating a comprehensive security plan is assessing your home's needs. This involves a thorough evaluation of your property and an understanding of potential risks.

- **Identify Vulnerable Areas:**

    - Walk around your home and property to identify areas vulnerable to intrusion.

    - Consider entry points like doors and windows, especially those on the ground floor, or easily accessible from the outside.

    - Look at other potential access points, such as garages, basements, and side gates.

- **Evaluate Current Security Measures:**

    - Take stock of your existing security measures, including locks, alarms, and cameras.

- Identify any gaps or weaknesses in your current system.

- **Consider Your Lifestyle:**

    - Think about your daily routines and how they impact your security needs.

    - Consider factors such as whether you travel frequently, have pets, or need to provide access to service personnel.

Step 2: Setting Security Goals

Once you have assessed your home's security needs, setting clear, achievable security goals is important. These goals will guide your decisions and help you prioritize your efforts.

- **Define Your Objectives:**

    - Decide what you want to achieve with your security plan. Examples include deterring potential intruders, ensuring the safety of family members, and protecting valuable possessions.

- **Set Priorities:**

    - Rank your security goals in order of importance. This will help you allocate resources and address the most critical areas first.

- **Establish Benchmarks:**

    - Determine how you will measure the success of your security plan. This might include reducing the number of false alarms, increasing the number of incidents captured on camera, or achieving a sense of peace of mind.

Step 3: Implementing Security Measures

With your goals in place, you can implement security measures to address your home's needs. This involves choosing the right equipment and strategies for each area of your property.

- **Securing Entry Points:**
    - Install high-quality locks on all doors and windows.
    - Consider adding deadbolts, strike plates, and security bars for extra protection.
    - Use doorbell cameras and intercom systems to monitor and control access to your home.

- **Enhancing Perimeter Security:**
    - Install outdoor cameras to cover key areas such as driveways, yards, and entryways.
    - Use motion-activated lights to deter intruders and improve visibility at night.
    - Consider installing fencing or gates to create a physical barrier around your property.

- **Improving Indoor Security:**
    - Place indoor cameras in common areas, hallways, and rooms with valuable items.

- Use smart locks and alarm systems to control access and provide alerts in case of unauthorized entry.

- Install sensors on doors and windows to detect and alert you to potential intrusions.

Step 4: Integrating Your Security System

Integrating your security system ensures that all components work together seamlessly. This can enhance the overall effectiveness of your security measures and make it easier to manage your system.

- **Centralize Control:**

    - Use a central control panel or smart home hub to manage all your security devices.

    - Ensure your cameras, alarms, locks, and sensors are compatible with your central control system.

- **Automate Security Routines:**

    - Set up automated routines to activate your security system based on your schedule or specific triggers.

    - Use geofencing to arm your system when you leave home and disarm it when you return.

- **Monitor and Respond:**

    - Use mobile apps to monitor your security system remotely and receive real-time alerts.

    - Establish a protocol for responding to alerts, including

contacting authorities or a security monitoring service.

Step 5: Educating Your Family

Ensuring everyone in your household understands the security plan and how to use the system is crucial. This helps prevent accidental alarms and provides a coordinated response in an emergency.

- **Train Family Members:**
    - Teach each family member how to use the security system, including arming/disarming the system and responding to alerts.
    - Show them how to operate any emergency features, such as panic buttons or two-way communication systems.

- **Establish Procedures:**
    - Create a family emergency plan that includes steps to take in case of a security breach.
    - Practice drills to ensure everyone knows what to do and where to go in an emergency.

Step 6: Regularly Reviewing and Updating Your Plan

Security needs can change over time, so it's important to regularly review and update your security plan to ensure its effectiveness.

- **Conduct Regular Audits:**
    - Periodically review your security system to ensure all

components are functioning correctly.

- Assess any changes to your property or lifestyle that might impact your security needs.

- **Stay Informed:**

  - Keep up with the latest security technologies and trends.
  - Consider upgrading your system or adding new features to address emerging threats.

- **Adjust Your Plan:**

  - Make adjustments to your security plan based on your regular audits and any new information.
  - Update your family on changes and ensure they understand new procedures or features.

Conclusion

Creating a comprehensive security plan tailored to your home's unique needs is essential for ensuring the safety and security of your family and property. You can build a robust and adaptable security strategy by assessing your security needs, setting clear goals, implementing effective measures, integrating your system, educating your family, and regularly reviewing your plan.

In the next chapter, we will explore how to stay vigilant and proactive in maintaining your home security, including tips for staying aware of potential threats and continuously improving your security measures. Together, we will continue to build a safer and more secure home.

Chapter 8: Staying Vigilant and Proactive in Home Security

The Importance of Ongoing Vigilance

Creating a comprehensive security plan and implementing advanced features are essential, but maintaining vigilance and being proactive in home security is equally important. Staying alert to potential threats and continuously improving your security measures can significantly enhance your home's protection. This chapter will explore strategies to help you remain vigilant and proactive in maintaining your home security.

Step 1: Staying Informed About Security Threats

Understanding the current security landscape and being aware of potential threats can help you take timely and effective measures to protect your home.

- **Monitor Local Crime Trends:**
    - **Stay Updated:** Regularly check local news, police reports, and community bulletins for information about crime trends in your area.
    - **Join Neighborhood Groups:** Participate in neighborhood watch programs or online community groups to share information and stay informed about suspicious activities.

- **Follow Security News:**
    - **Read Security Blogs:** Subscribe to blogs and websites focusing on home security to stay updated on the latest threats and security technologies.
    - **Follow Experts:** Follow security experts and organizations on social media for real-time updates and advice.

- **Learn from Incidents:**
    - **Analyze Break-Ins:** Study incidents of break-ins or attempted burglaries in your area to understand common tactics used by intruders.
    - **Apply Lessons:** Use the information to enhance your security measures and prevent similar incidents from happening to your home.

Step 2: Regularly Updating Your Security System

Keeping your security system updated ensures it remains effective against new threats.

- **Software and Firmware Updates:**

    - **Automatic Updates:** Enable automatic updates for your security cameras, smart locks, and other devices to ensure they have the latest features and security patches.

    - **Manual Checks:** Regularly check for updates and install them promptly if automatic updates are unavailable.

- **Upgrade Hardware:**

    - **Assess Performance:** Periodically evaluate the performance of your security devices and consider upgrading to newer models with advanced features.

    - **Replace Outdated Equipment:** Replace any outdated or malfunctioning equipment to maintain optimal security coverage.

- **Expand Your System:**

    - **Add New Devices:** To enhance your system's capabilities, consider adding new security devices such as additional cameras, sensors, or smart home integrations.

    - **Integrate New Technologies:** Stay informed about emerging security technologies and integrate them into your system as needed.

Step 3: Conducting Regular Security Audits

Regular security audits help identify weaknesses in your system and ensure that all components function correctly.

- **Perform Inspections:**
  - **Visual Checks:** Regularly inspect all security devices for wear, damage, or tampering signs.
  - **Functional Tests:** Test the functionality of cameras, alarms, locks, and other devices to ensure they work correctly.

- **Review Coverage:**
  - **Assess Coverage Areas:** Verify that your security cameras and sensors adequately cover all critical areas of your property.
  - **Adjust Angles:** Adjust camera angles and sensor positions to eliminate blind spots and improve coverage.

- **Evaluate Effectiveness:**
  - **Analyze Data:** Review security footage and logs to assess your system's effectiveness and identify any gaps or issues.
  - **Solicit Feedback:** Ask family members for feedback on the security system's performance and ease of use.

Step 4: Enhancing Physical Security Measures

In addition to electronic security devices, physical security measures play a crucial role in protecting your home.

- **Strengthen Entry Points:**
  - **Reinforce Doors and Windows:** Install reinforced doors, security bars, and shatterproof film on windows to make entry points more resistant to forced entry.
  - **Secure Locks:** Use high-quality deadbolts and smart locks to enhance the security of doors and windows.

- **Improve Outdoor Security:**
  - **Lighting:** Install motion-activated lights around your property to deter intruders and improve visibility.
  - **Fencing and Gates:** Use sturdy fencing and secure gates to create a physical barrier around your property.

- **Landscaping:**
  - **Trim Vegetation:** Keep bushes and trees trimmed to eliminate hiding spots for intruders.
  - **Defensive Planting:** Consider planting thorny or dense shrubs near windows and fences to deter intruders.

Step 5: Educating Your Family and Staying Engaged

Keeping your family informed and engaged in home security practices is essential for maintaining a secure environment.

- **Conduct Training:**

    - **Teach Basics:** Ensure all family members know how to use the security system, including arming/disarming alarms and accessing camera feeds.

    - **Emergency Procedures:** Create and practice emergency plans, including what to do in case of a break-in or security breach.

- **Promote Awareness:**

    - **Encourage Vigilance:** Encourage family members to stay vigilant and report any suspicious activities or potential security issues.

    - **Share Updates:** Keep everyone informed about any changes or updates to the security system and procedures.

- **Involve Everyone:**

    - **Assign Roles:** Assign specific security roles to family members, such as checking locks at night or monitoring security feeds during travel.

    - **Foster a Security Mindset:** Cultivate a proactive security mindset within the family, emphasizing the importance of ongoing vigilance and participation.

Conclusion

Staying vigilant and proactive in maintaining your home security is vital for ensuring long-term protection. You can create a secure and resilient home environment by staying informed about potential threats, regularly updating and auditing your security system, enhancing physical security measures, and educating your family.

The next chapter will discuss strategies for responding to security breaches and emergencies, ensuring you and your family are prepared to handle any situation effectively. Together, we will continue to build a safer and more secure home.

Chapter 9: Responding to Security Breaches and Emergencies

Being Prepared for the Unexpected

Despite your best efforts to secure your home, security breaches and emergencies can still occur. Knowing how to respond effectively can make a significant difference in protecting your family and property. This final chapter will discuss strategies for handling security breaches, preparing for emergencies, and ensuring that you and your family are ready to act swiftly and appropriately.

Step 1: Recognizing Security Breaches

The first step in responding to a security breach is recognizing the signs of an intrusion or potential threat.

- **Common Indicators of a Security Breach:**
    - Alarms: A triggered alarm from your security system.
    - Unexpected Notifications: Alerts from your security cameras or smart home devices indicating unusual activity.
    - Physical Signs: Broken windows, damaged doors, or other signs of forced entry.
- **Immediate Actions:**
    - Stay Calm: Keep a clear head to assess the situation accurately.
    - Verify Alerts: Use your security system's app or control panel to verify the alert and check camera feeds for unusual activity.
    - Avoid Confrontation: If you suspect an intruder is inside your home, do not confront them. Instead, follow your emergency plan.

Step 2: Implementing Your Emergency Plan

A well-thought-out emergency plan ensures everyone knows what to do in a security breach.
- **Creating an Emergency Plan:**
    - Designate Safe Zones: Identify safe areas in your home where family members can go in an emergency.

- **Establish Communication:** Ensure everyone knows how to contact emergency services and each other.

- **Plan Escape Routes:** If evacuation is necessary, map out multiple escape routes from each room.

- Executing the Plan:
  - **Gather in Safe Zones:** Move to the designated safe areas and lock the doors.
  - **Contact Authorities:** Call 911 or your local emergency number to report the breach and request assistance.
  - **Stay Quiet:** Keep noise to a minimum to avoid attracting the intruder's attention.

- Practice Regularly:
  - **Drills:** Conduct regular drills to ensure everyone knows their roles and the emergency plan.
  - **Review and Update:** Review and update the plan to account for any changes in home or family dynamics.

Step 3: Handling Different Types of Emergencies

Different emergencies require different responses. Here are some guidelines for handling various scenarios:

- Burglary:
  - **Immediate Action:** Follow your emergency plan and contact authorities.

- **Post-Incident:** Document any stolen or damaged property and inform the police. Notify your insurance company to file a claim.

- **Fire:**

  - **Immediate Action:** Evacuate the home immediately using designated escape routes. Call 911, and do not attempt to re-enter.

  - **Post-Incident:** Once it's safe, document the damage and contact your insurance company. If necessary, arrange for temporary housing.

- **Medical Emergencies:**

  - **Immediate Action:** Call 911 and provide first aid if trained. Use any medical alert systems if available.

  - **Post-Incident:** Follow up with healthcare providers and ensure all medical records are updated.

- **Natural Disasters:**

  - **Immediate Action:** Follow local emergency guidelines and evacuate if necessary. Use your emergency kit and stay informed through local news and alerts.

  - **Post-Incident:** Assess the damage to your home and contact your insurance company. If needed, seek assistance from local disaster relief organizations.

Step 4: Post-Incident Recovery and Prevention

After dealing with an emergency, it's important to focus on recovery and take steps to prevent future incidents.

- **Recovery Steps:**

    - **Assess Damage:** Carefully inspect your home for any damage or missing items.

    - **Document Everything:** Take photos and write detailed descriptions of all damage and losses.

    - **Contact Insurance:** File claims with your insurance company as soon as possible.

- **Strengthen Security Measures:**

    - **Review the Incident:** Analyze how the breach occurred and identify any weaknesses in your security system.

    - **Upgrade Security:** Consider upgrading your security system with additional cameras, sensors, or advanced features.

    - **Community Support:** Share your experience with neighbors and community groups to raise awareness and encourage collective vigilance.

Step 5: Emotional and Psychological Support

Experiencing a security breach or emergency can be traumatic. Addressing the emotional and psychological impact on you and your family is essential.

- **Seek Professional Help:**

    - **Counseling:** Consider seeking counseling or therapy for family members affected by the incident.

    - **Support Groups:** Join local or online support groups for people who have experienced similar incidents.

- **Rebuild a Sense of Security:**

    - **Routine:** Establish a routine to restore normalcy and a sense of control.

    - **Engage in Positive Activities:** Participate in activities that promote relaxation and well-being.

Conclusion

Responding effectively to security breaches and emergencies is crucial to maintaining a secure home. By recognizing potential threats, implementing a solid emergency plan, handling different types of emergencies appropriately, and focusing on recovery and prevention, you can ensure that your home remains a haven for your family.

Conclusion

In "The Complete Security Camera Handbook: Planning, Implementation, and Preparedness for a Safe Home," we've embarked on a comprehensive journey to fortify your home security through strategic planning, effective implementation, and proactive preparedness. This book has aimed to equip you with the knowledge and tools necessary to create a robust security system tailored to your unique needs.

We began by understanding the critical importance of proper camera placement, delving into the different types of security cameras and their optimal uses. This foundational knowledge set the stage for mapping out your home and identifying key areas that require vigilant monitoring. From entry points to common indoor areas, we've covered it all to ensure no blind spots are left unprotected.

The installation chapter provided practical, step-by-step guidance on setting up your security cameras, ensuring they are correctly mounted and configured for maximum efficiency. We then explored various recording options, from local storage to cloud solutions, helping you choose the best method to capture and store vital footage.

Regular maintenance and troubleshooting are essential to keep your security system in top shape. This book detailed how to maintain your cameras and offered solutions to common problems, ensuring your system remains reliable and effective. Furthermore, we discussed advanced features and integrations, such as motion detection and smart home connectivity, to enhance your security system's functionality.

Another critical focus was creating a comprehensive security plan tailored to your home. By assessing your needs, setting clear goals, and implementing effective measures, you can build a robust defense against potential threats. Staying vigilant and proactive was emphasized to continually adapt and improve your security measures.

Finally, we addressed how to respond to security breaches and emergencies, providing you with strategies to handle different scenarios and ensure your family's safety.

As we conclude this handbook, it's crucial to remember that security is an ongoing process. Regularly review and update your security plan, stay informed about new technologies, and remain vigilant. Your proactive efforts will go a long way in protecting your home and loved ones.

Call to Action

Now that you have the knowledge and tools from "The Complete Security Camera Handbook," it's time to implement this information. Start by assessing your current security setup and identifying areas for improvement. Implement the strategies and tips this book outlines to enhance your home security systematically.

Stay engaged with your community, share your insights, and encourage collective vigilance. A secure neighborhood benefits everyone.

Continuously educate yourself about the latest security advancements and integrate new technologies to stay ahead of potential threats.

Your journey to a safer home doesn't end here. Keep this handbook as a reference, revisit the chapters as needed, and adapt your security measures to evolving circumstances. By taking these proactive steps, you can ensure a secure and peaceful environment for your family.

Thank you for trusting us to guide you on this important journey. Stay safe, stay vigilant, and continue to protect what matters most. We can build a safer world, one home at a time.

We Appreciate Your Feedback!

Thank you for reading *The Complete Security Camera Handbook: Planning, Implementation, and Preparedness for a Safe Home*. We hope this book has provided you with valuable insights and practical advice to help you secure your home effectively.

Your feedback is incredibly important to us and helps us continue improving our content to serve readers like you better. If you found this book helpful, we would be grateful if you could take a moment to leave a review.

Here's how you can help:
1. **Share Your Experience:**

    - How did this book help you better understand and implement your home security system?

    - Were the instructions clear, practical, and easy to follow?

    - Did the book meet your expectations in terms of content and usability?

2. **Leave a Review:**

    - Visit the platform where you purchased this book (such as Amazon, Goodreads, or another retailer) and leave your honest review.

    - Your feedback helps us improve and helps other readers make informed decisions about their home security needs.

3. **Spread the Word:**

- If you know someone who might benefit from this guide, please share it with them. Personal recommendations go a long way in helping others discover useful resources.

Your Support Matters

Your review not only helps us grow but also contributes to the community of readers who are looking for trustworthy and practical guidance on home security. Whether you leave a brief comment or a detailed review, every bit of feedback is appreciated and valued.

What's Next?

We'd love to hear from you if you have any suggestions for future content or ideas on how we can improve. Feel free to reach out with your thoughts.

Again, Thank you for your support and for being a part of our journey towards safer homes. We look forward to your feedback and hope to continue serving you with more insightful content in the future.

Stay safe, stay vigilant, and thank you for your time!

Best regards,

L.G. Schreyer